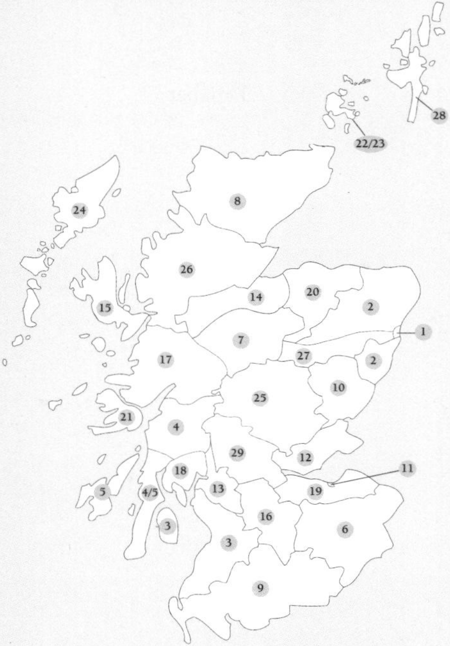

1. Aberdeen
2. Aberdeenshire
3. Arran & Ayrshire
4. Argyll
5. Southern Argyll
6. The Borders
7. The Cairngorms
8. Caithness & Sutherland
9. Dumfries and Galloway
10. Dundee & Angus
11. Edinburgh
12. Fife, Kinross & Clackmannan
13. Glasgow
14. Inverness
15. The Isle of Skye
16. Lanarkshire
17. Lochaber
18. Loch Lomond, Cowal & Bute
19. The Lothians
20. Moray
21. Mull & Iona
22. Orkney
23. Orkney in Wartime
24. The Outer Hebrides
25. Perthshire
26. Ross & Cromarty
27. Royal Deeside
28. Shetland
29. Stirling & The Trossachs

The remaining four books, Caledonia, Distinguished Distilleries, Scotland's Mountains and Scotland's Wildlife feature locations throughout the country so are not included in the above list.

PICTURING SCOTLAND

GLASGOW

NESS PUBLISHING

2 A view from Fereneze Braes in East Renfrewshire that looks north right over Glasgow to the mountains around and beyond Loch Lomond.

GLASGOW

Welcome to Glasgow!

Scotland's greatest city is something of an enigma: the one-time industrial heart of the British Empire that became the 1990 European City of Culture; its foundation was ecclesiastical, yet its spiritual power-base had declined long before its economic growth took off. And although this growth was based on international trade, it does not have a natural harbour. The reason for the city's success comes down to its ability to adapt to changing circumstances and exploit the opportunities presented. As this book will show, the different phases in the city's historical timeline can be traced from east to west, beginning with medieval remnants at and around the Cathedral, then flowing westwards with the river to the ultra-modern structures that define the post-industrial rebirth that has taken place along the River Clyde.

Glasgow grew up on the banks of the Clyde at one of its shallowest crossing points. Celtic druids were among the first people to have settled along the Clyde, although the Romans also established forts in the area during their attempts to colonise Scotland. Archaeological evidence shows that the earliest settlements in the area were fishing communities, with salmon and herring being the main catches. It was into this primitive environment that Glasgow's founding father arrived sometime around AD543. That notion was probably not in Kentigern's mind when he established a church on the banks of the Molendinar burn (a tributary of the Clyde) approximately where Glasgow Cathedral (opposite) now stands. Kentigern acquired the nickname Mungo,

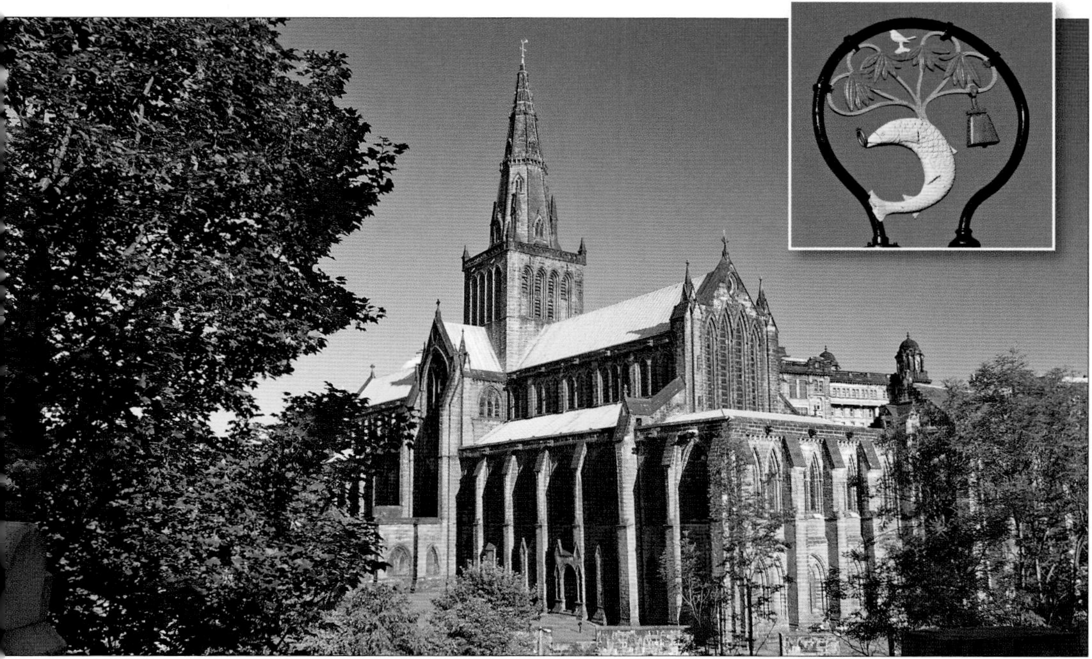

Glasgow Cathedral. Built during the 13th to 15th centuries, it is the only medieval cathedral on the Scottish mainland to have survived the 1560 Reformation virtually complete. Inset: Glasgow Coat of Arms.

meaning 'dear one' and 'St Mungo' has long been a soubriquet for Glasgow.

Glasgow's coat of arms (see inset on previous page) represents miraculous works credited to St Kentigern. The bird: as a boy under the tutelage of St Serf in the monastery at Culross, it is said that he brought St Serf's pet robin back to life after it was killed by some of the other acolytes. The tree, from which hangs Kentigern's bell, stands for the branch which he caused to ignite miraculously after the monastery's holy fire had been mischievously extinguished. The fish relates to a story about Queen Languoreth, suspected of giving her wedding ring to a lover; but the ring mysteriously appeared in the stomach of a salmon caught by Kentigern's monks.

Little is known of Glasgow's development between Kentigern's death and its establishment as an Episcopal See in 1115. From that moment the combination of religious authority and associated land wealth provided a firm platform for growth. In the late 12th century, King William the Lion issued a charter which granted a large

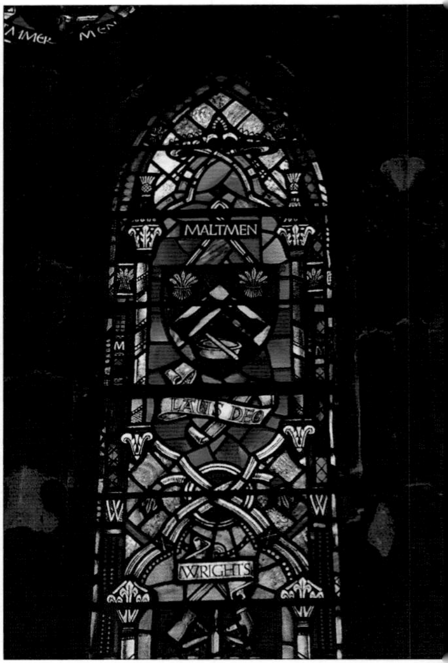

Stained-glass window in Glasgow Cathedral honouring two of the city's trades

area of land to the Bishops of Glasgow and also gave them the right to set up a burgh in Glasgow. The main privilege arising from this, and an extremely valuable one at the time, was the right to hold a market. Soon Glasgow's merchants dominated all of the trade in the Clyde Valley area. Its position was further enhanced in 1450 when James II issued a charter that gave Glasgow the status of a Royal Burgh, even though it did not officially own that title. The University of Glasgow was founded the following year.

Up until the early 16th century, Glasgow maintained its dominant position as both an academic and an ecclesiastical centre. However, the Reformation in Scotland allowed Glasgow merchants and craftsmen to flourish: the virtual eradication of Roman Catholic Church hegemony enabled a corresponding increase in civic power. The city's motto – 'Let Glasgow flourish' was powerfully fulfilled, leaving the legacy of the fine metropolis we shall explore.

The St Mungo Museum of Religious Life and Art is situated close to Glasgow Cathedral.

8 Glasgow Green lies about half-a-mile south of the Cathedral district and underlines the appropriateness of the city's name: Glasgow ('glas-cu') means 'dear green place'. This panorama shows the layout

of its main structures: on the left is the Doulton Fountain with Templeton's Carpet Factory behind, while the People's Palace is on the right. We shall return for a closer look at each of these later.

10 St Mungo's Chapel is located in the extensive and highly atmospheric undercroft of Glasgow Cathedral. St Mungo was buried here – opinions about the date of his death vary from 603 to 614.

On the hill to the east of the Cathedral is the Glasgow Necropolis. Commissioned in 1828 and holding its first burial in 1832, it contains around 3,500 tombs, many of which have to be seen to be believed.

12 Just across Castle Street from the Cathedral is Provand's Lordship. Originally built in 1471 as an alms-house, it is the oldest surviving house in Glasgow. Also seen here at the rear of the building is the

St Nicholas Garden, a walled 'physic' garden containing many examples of plants that were in common use in the 15th century. Above: Cuthbert Simson's Room, beautifully recreated in Provand's Lordship.

14 The Doulton Fountain was gifted to the city by Sir Henry Doulton and unveiled in 1888. A sculptural extravaganza, at 14m/46ft high and 21m/70ft across the base, it is the largest terracotta fountain in the world.

The stunning façade of the former Templeton's Carpet Factory, with its multi-coloured brickwork, mosaic panels and marble columns, is directly inspired by the Doge's Palace in Venice. Built 1888-1892.

16 Opened in 1898, the People's Palace and Winter Garden had reading and recreation rooms on the ground floor, a museum on the first floor and an art gallery above it. This combination of facilities was

very much in tune with Victorian aspirations to provide working class people with opportunities for self-improvement and decorous, sober leisure activity. Above: a variety of flora in the People's Palace.

18 The McLennan Arch stands at the north-western (city) end of Glasgow Green and provides a spectacular entry to the park. The Nelson column of 1806 can be seen in the distance.

Leaving Glasgow Green and heading west into the city centre brings us to Glasgow Cross, the focal point of an earlier period in the city's history. On the right (illuminated) is the 1922-built Mercat Building.

20 Left: Glasgow Cross marks the south-eastern corner of the Merchant City and is the location of the Tolbooth Steeple which dates to 1627. Right: nearby, this tower is all that remains of the Tron Kirk.

Continuing westwards to St Enoch Square, this contrast in styles catches the eye. On the left is an Art Deco bank building and on the right the original St Enoch Subway station building.

22 Argyle Street, where it is crossed by the platforms of Glasgow Central station. The space underneath was nicknamed 'The Highland man's umbrella' as it provided shelter for men who came south to work.

Ever a hive of activity, this is the concourse of Central Station, notable for the amount of attractive wooden architecture that survives from an earlier era. The Champagne Bar is part of the Central Hotel.

24 In the city centre at Exchange Place is one of Glasgow's finest Art Deco interiors. In 1935, Rogano was refitted in the same style as the Cunard liner *Queen Mary* and retains this exquisite appearance today.

Exchange Place leads to the 1829-built Royal Exchange in its fine square, a grand edifice where business transactions took place. The rear end of the building is seen here under a 'ceiling' of Christmas lights.

26 This is the front of the Royal Exchange which today houses the Gallery of Modern Art, the most-visited modern art gallery in Scotland. The statue is of the Duke of Wellington.

Laid out in 1801, George Square is right at the heart of the city. Glasgow's magnificent City Chambers stands at the far end. Built from 1883 to 1888 in the Italian Renaissance style, it is one . . .

28 . . . of the finest public buildings of 19th-century Britain. Even at the back it retains its finesse – the archways seen here span John Street and connect it to the City Chambers extension.

For all the grandeur of the exterior, it is the interior that really takes the breath away – no visit to Glasgow is complete without doing the tour! It has appeared in films as the Vatican and the Kremlin!

30 Left: George Square is full of statues. The tallest is that of Sir Walter Scott, seen looking down on Lieutenant General Sir John Moore. Right: the spire of Hutcheson's Hall in the Merchant City.

Created around 1750 as a planned development on a grid pattern, Merchant City's opulent buildings reflect the wealth generated by Glasgow's tobacco-based 18th-C. trade boom. The City Halls are a good example.

32 This elaborately sculpted peacock sits above Princes Square Mall on Buchanan Street, one of Glasgow's principal shopping streets. It runs south to north from Argyle Street up to Buchanan Galleries.

And right at the top of Buchanan Street, outside the Galleries, Scotland's first First Minister Donald Dewar stands in sculpted serenity in front of the Glasgow Royal Concert Hall.

34 Glasgow has grown in a westerly direction and here, on Wellington Street, is a scene which typifies the effect produced by modern, glass-panelled office blocks – reflections galore!

Running west from the north end of Buchanan St., Sauchiehall Street is the location of the famous Willow Tea Rooms, designed by Charles Rennie Mackintosh. Left: exterior. Right: interior details.

36 Left: further along Sauchiehall Street and now known as Baird Hall, this Art Deco tower was built as the Beresford Hotel in the 1930s. Right: the entrance to the Glasgow School of Art on Renfrew Stree

The School of Art's building is one of the great works of Glasgow architect, designer, artist and alumnus Charles Rennie Mackintosh (1868–1928). His style, as exemplified in this picture of the Library, . . .

38 . . . is applied to all aspects of the building from structure to furnishings, resulting in a wonderful fusion of his disciplines. Left: the main stairwell. Right: one of many stained-glass windows.

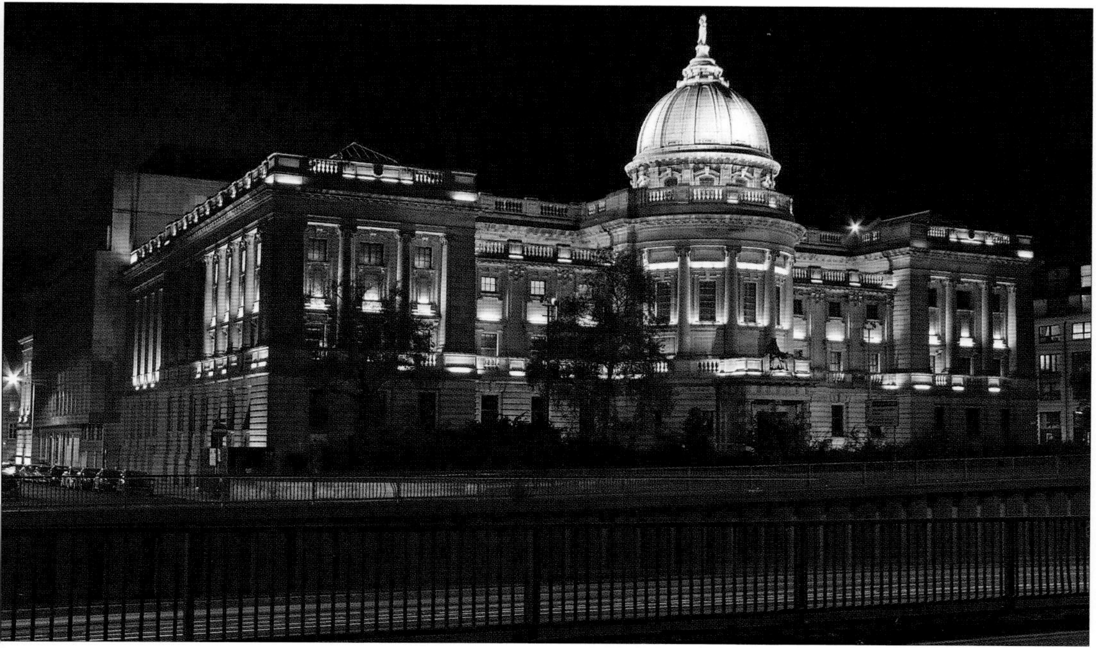

Further west again, in the Charing Cross district, is the Mitchell Library, one of the largest public reference libraries in Europe. One of Glasgow's best-loved buildings, it looks especially impressive by night.

40 Now a brief diversion for a first look at the River Clyde. This stretch of the river has undergone a radical transformation from shipyards to avant-garde architectural hotspot. On the left is the Scottish

:xhibition & Conference Centre's Clyde Auditorium, while on the right is the new 12,000-seat SSE
Hydro arena. The SECC precinct forms the largest venue of the Glasgow 2014 Commonwealth Games.

42 Glasgow's West End begins at Charing Cross and features some of the city's finest suburban architecture. The stylish layout of Park Circus and Park Quadrant is seen to good advantage in this aerial view.

Left: The Great Western Road at Kelvinbridge with the needle-like spire of Lansdowne Church beyond. Right: a little further along Great Western Road are the Glasgow Botanic Gardens.

44 Centrepiece of the Botanic Gardens is Kibble's Palace Glasshouse, an 'A'-listed 19th century, curvilinear iron structure of exquisite design and form. The Gardens are known internationally for their

extensive tropical and temperate plant collections from around the world, some of which can be seen in this interior view. The structure is named after its creator, John Kibble of Coulport, Loch Long.

46 From the 'Botanics', a southwards stroll down Byres Road leads to Glasgow University.
Left: the University bell tower, a prominent Glasgow landmark. Right: a close-up view of its spire.

Founded in 1451, the University of Glasgow has been on this site since 1870 and was designed by Sir George Gilbert Scott. This superb colonnade underneath Bute Hall exemplifies the Gothic Revival Style.

48 The colonnade (or open undercroft) sits between two large quads, this being the one on the west. The campus contains more listed buildings than any other Scottish university.

Seen in silhouette at sundown, the university takes on the look of a fantasy castle.

50 In the cold light of a snowy day, this view shows the spatial relationship between the university up on Gilmorehill and our next destination, Kelvingrove, the twin towers of which can be seen on the left.

This statue of William Thomson (1824-1907), 1st Baron Kelvin and one of the most famous scientists of his age, stands in Kelvingrove Park. His title is derived from the River Kelvin.

WORKS·INAUGURATED·BY·QUEEN·VICTORIA·14TH·OCTOBER·1859

52 Many of Glasgow's statues and fountains also feature finely crafted low-relief panels. This one is a good example, adorning the Victoria Fountain in Kelvingrove Park. Glasgow Cathedral can be seen in the centre.

Kelvingrove Art Gallery and Museum stands at the western end of the park and makes a truly spectacular sight at night. However, its popularity has more to do with the 8,000 exhibits on show.

54 With so much to see *in* Kelvingrove, it's easy to forget to look *at* the building itself, which deserves careful examination. This is the Centre Hall, with its magnificent organ which is played most days.

Here, in one of the larger of the 22 themed, state-of-the-art galleries, the sheer range of the exhibits can be appreciated. The aeroplane is a real Spitfire!

56 Now we turn our attention to the Clyde for a more thorough investigation of this great river. Looking west, on the left are the cranes at what is now BAE Systems Surface Ships at Govan, better

nown in former times as Fairfields Shipyard. To the right, the tops of the masts of the *Glenlee* see p.64) rise above new blocks of flats.

58 Looking upriver from Broomielaw, no fewer than five bridges can be seen: nearest is Tradeston Bridge, then George IV Bridge, railway bridge, Glasgow Bridge and a fragment of Portland Street suspension bridge.

Here, just before dawn, we see Tradeston Bridge illuminated. This new footbridge, opened in 2009, has earned the nickname 'Squiggly Bridge' due to its unusual, curving 'S' shape.

60 Now moving downriver, here is more evidence of Glasgow's riverside regeneration in the form of this rather beautifully curved and glass-fronted office block at Anderston Quay.

he 140m Clyde Arc or 'Squinty' Bridge frames the Finnieston Crane and joins Finnieston on the north bank with Pacific Quay on the south. The bridge is built on the skew, hence the 'squinty' nickname.

62 Pacific Quay is home to the Glasgow Science Centre, another example of cutting-edge architecture. It is a major visitor attraction, presenting scientific and technological concepts in unique and inspiring ways

Glasgow's newest museum is the Riverside. On the north bank of the Clyde in Partick, its glass façade ces the river, reflecting the *Glenlee*, one of only five Clyde-built sailing vessels afloat in the world today.

64 The Riverside Museum brilliantly showcases the transport, engineering and shipbuilding legacy that mad
Glasgow great. And in a number of mirrors it presents fascinatingly quirky reflections of the vicinity.

One of its highlights is this wonderfully atmospheric recreation of a Glasgow street of a century ago. And are those apparitions perhaps ghosts from that time, taking a nostalgic look at their own past?!

66 Panoramic views can now be enjoyed from the top of the Titan Crane at Clydebank. Completed in 1907, its 150-ton capacity was capable of lifting the heaviest components into newly built ships.

Visitors travel by lift to the top of the crane and can inspect its workings, as well as looking down on passing shipping.

68 Continuing downstream, Dumbarton Rock towers above the Clyde estuary, with Dumbarton Castle enjoying a commanding view over the waters. Dumbarton was the centre of the ancient kingdom of Strathclyde.

Also in Dumbarton is the Denny Ship Model Experiment Tank – step back into the world of the Victorian ship designer! Built in 1882, it retains many original features including the 300 foot-long test tank.

70 Our furthest point on this leg of the journey is the southern end of Loch Lomond at Balloch. Left: the *Maid of the Loch*. Right: Drumkinnon Tower, home of Loch Lomond Sea Life Aquarium.

An evening stroll from Balloch along the banks of the River Leven soon reveals Loch Lomond stretching out as far as the eye can see to the north, and with views across the loch like this.

72 This aerial panorama shows Loch Lomond in full winter splendour, with Ben Lomond in the distance. By area, it is Britain's largest inland loch, covering some 71,000,000m² (that's 27.5 square miles), with

an average depth of 37m/121ft. Its greatest depth however is 190m/623ft. The loch contains a staggering 2,600,000,000m^3 of water! As can be seen, it has many islands (37 in all), some of which are inhabited.

74 Now we turn our attention to Glasgow south of the Clyde. Bellahouston Park in the south-west of the city has much of interest; the Walled Garden, seen here, is particularly fine.

Just outside the Walled Garden stands the House for an Art Lover. Designed by Charles Rennie Mackintosh in 1901, it was only built in the 1990s and is a great draw for Mackintosh devotees.

76 Just south of Bellahouston Park is the extensive Pollok Country Park, at the centre of which is Pollok House. Designed by William Adam and built from 1742 to 1752, the side pavilions were added in 1890.

The sumptuous mahogany and marble entrance hall of Pollok House.

Shipping magnate William Burrell amassed an astonishing collection of over 8,000 artefacts. It is housed in a purpose-built gallery in Pollok Park. Above is the reconstruction of the Drawing Room from Burrell's own home, Hutton Castle.

78 The White Cart River runs through Pollok Country Park and helps to create some wonderfully rural scenes. This old watermill is next to the Pollok House stables.

Holmwood House is in the south-side suburb of Cathcart. The work of one of Glasgow's most notable architects, Alexander 'Greek' Thomson, this villa was built in 1857-8 for a local mill owner.

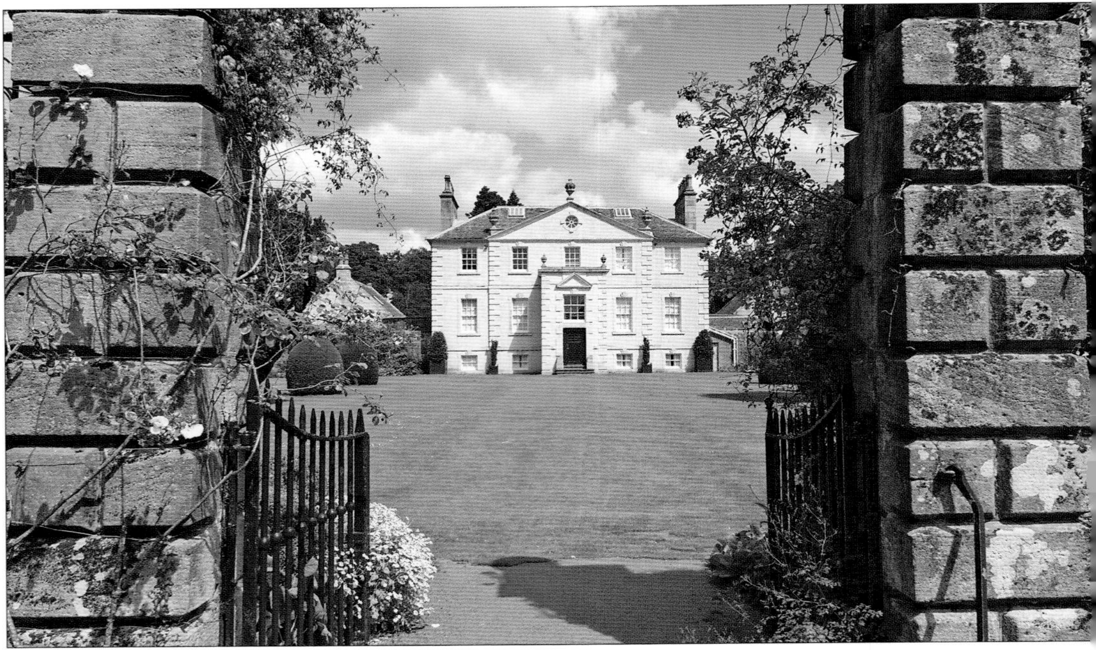

80 Continuing south from Cathcart and crossing into East Renfrewshire, we arrive at Greenbank Garden in Clarkston. Here, Greenbank House is viewed from the entrance to the Walled Garden.

This contains many treasures, including (left) this beautifully elegant fountain, a huge variety of plants and some wonderful topiary, a highlight of which is this huge owl.

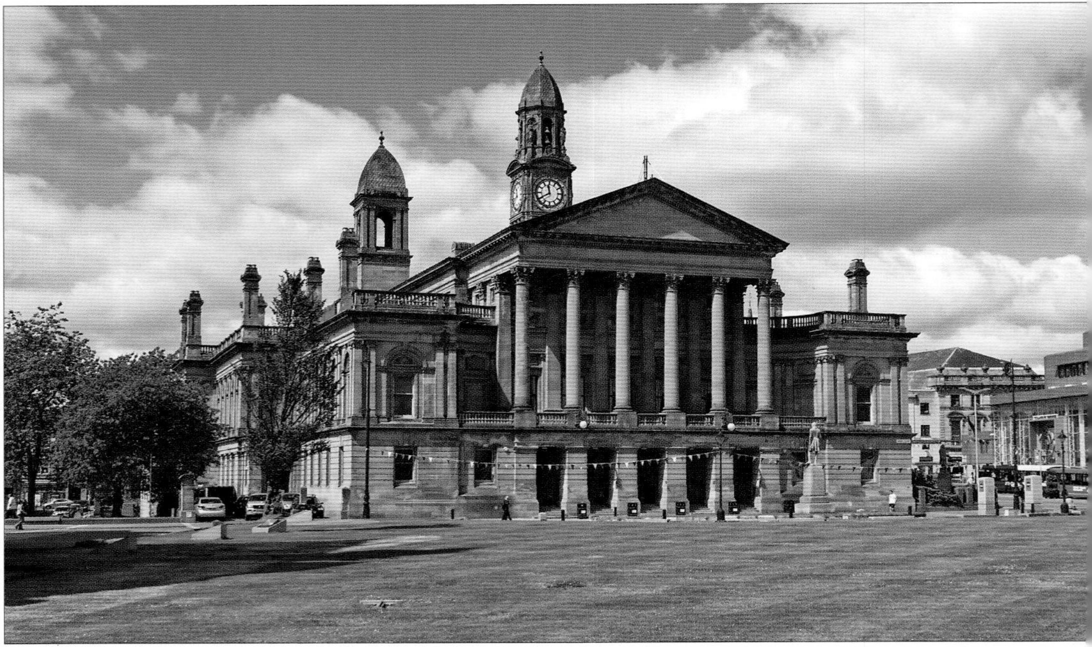

82 Moving west into Renfrewshire, this is Paisley's very fine Town Hall. Paisley grew from the 17th century as a textiles town and the Town Hall was funded by one the town's leading thread manufacturers.

Industrial money underpinned the development of Paisley in many ways, helping to create a pleasing town centre. The statue commemorates the reign of Queen Victoria. Inset: Paisley Corporation coat of arms.

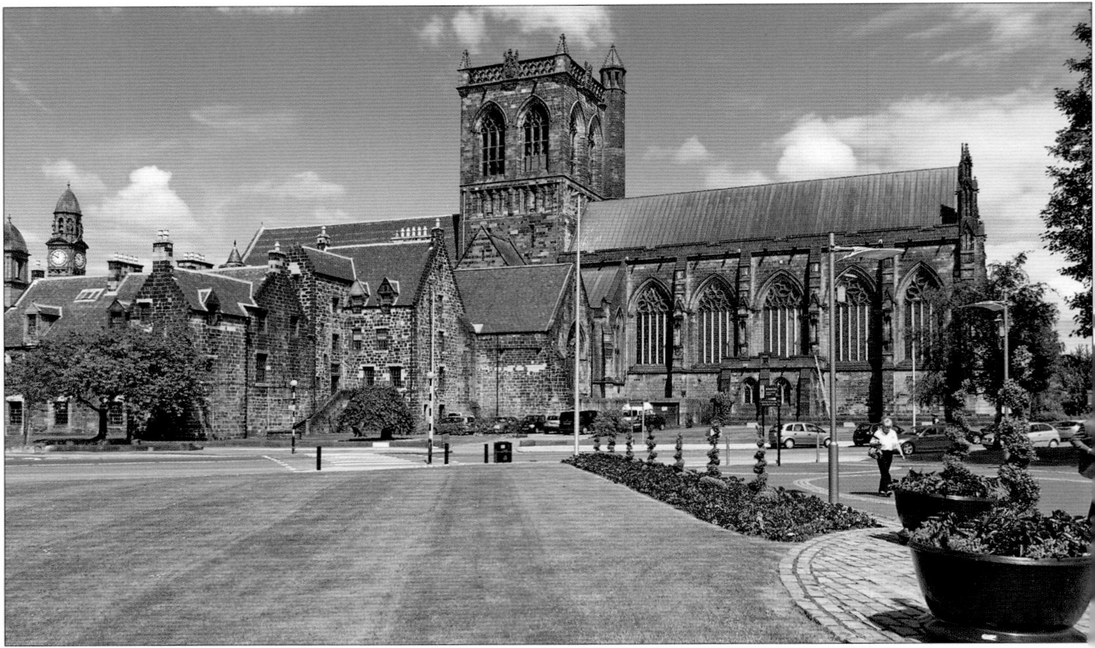

84 Paisley's roots go back to the 6th century when St Mirin established a church, around which a settlement grew up. Its ecclesiastical importance was consolidated by the founding of the abbey, seen here, in 1163.

Paisley Abbey's fine condition is the product of almost continuous restoration from the 1860s onwards. This is the view of the choir, altar and east window. Unusually, the choir is longer than the nave.

86 Not far from Paisley is the village of Kilbarchan, where a weaver's cottage of 1723 vintage has been preserved, complete with working handloom, the last one of 800 that used to operate in the village.

North-west of Kilbarchan and over into Inverclyde not far from Kilmacolm is Knapps Loch. Seen here on a frosty winter day, this little-known stretch of water is a gem of a scene.

88 Returning briefly to Glasgow for one last look at the Clyde, this evening panorama shows, from left to right, the Crowne Plaza Hotel, Clyde Auditorium, Finnieston Crane, various bridges,

the BBC Scotland building and the Science Centre.

90 Finlaystone Country Estate stands above the Clyde near the Renfrewshire/Inverclyde border. As well as the formal gardens and house seen here, there are woodland walks and play areas.

Greenock became Scotland's major west-coast port due to its role as Glasgow's port until the Clyde was dredged upstream. Centre-stage is the 75m/245ft Victoria Tower, part of Greenock's municipal buildings.

92 Greenock is a host port when the Tall Ships race comes to Scottish waters. The many masts of these fine vessels give an idea of what the port would have looked like in the 18th and 19th centuries.

The preserved paddle steamer *Waverley* plies the Clyde estuary during the summer and is popular with the many folk who enjoy sailing 'doon the watter'. Here she accelerates powerfully away from Greenock Pier.

94 A change of transport mode now as we reach our final destination by train at Wemyss Bay station. It is well worth seeing for its flamboyant, stylish construction and because generations of Glaswegians

have come this way to catch the boat for the Isle of Bute. Turn your back on the picture opposite and head down the broad passage (left) to the ferry terminal (right). But that's another journey . . .

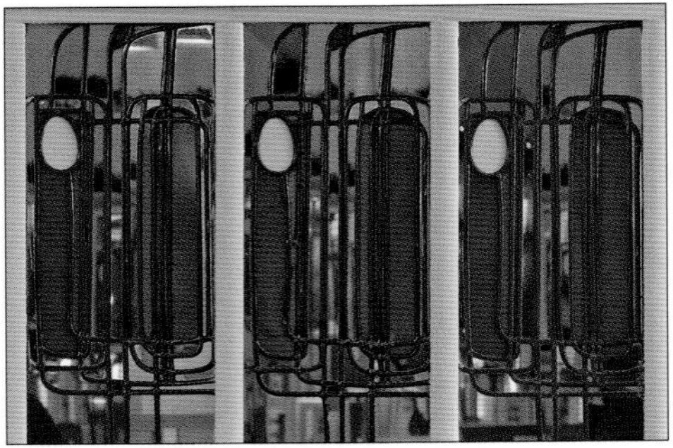

Published 2012 by Ness Publishing, 47 Academy Street, Elgin, Moray, IV30 1LR. Reprinted 2014, 2015 & 2016.
Phone 01343 549663 www.nesspublishing.co.uk

ISBN 978-1-906549-20-6

Front cover: George Square; p.1: statue of St Kentigern at Kelvingrove Art Gallery and Museum; p.4: Sophy Cave 'head' at Kelvingrove Art Gallery and Museum; this page: mirror detail at Willow Tea Rooms; back cover: Riverside Museum.

For a list of websites and phone numbers please turn over >

Websites and phone numbers (where available) for principal places featured in this book in order of appearance:

Glasgow Cathedral: www.glasgowcathedral.org.uk (T) 0141 552 8198
Glasgow Green: www.glasgow.gov.uk
Glasgow Necropolis: www.glasgownecropolis.org (T) 0141 287 3961
Provand's Lordship: www.glasgowlife.org.uk (T) 0141 552 8819
Doulton Fountain: www.glasgow.gov.uk
Templeton's Carpet Factory: www.clydewaterfrontheritage.com
People's Palace: www.clydewaterfrontheritage.com (T) 0141 271 2951
Glasgow Cross: www.scotland-guide.co.uk
Rogano www.roganoglasgow.com (T) 0141 248 4055
Royal Exchange: www.scotcities.com/central
Museum of Modern Art: www.glasgowlife.org.uk (T) 0141 287 3050
City Chambers: www.glasgow.gov.uk (T) 0141 287 4018 (for guided tours)
Merchant City: www.glasgowmerchantcity.net
Royal Concert Hall: www.glasgowconcerthalls.com (T) 0141 353 8000
Willow Tea Rooms: www.willowtearooms.co.uk (T) 0141 332 0521
Glasgow School of Art: www.gsa.ac.uk (T) 0141 353 4530
Clyde Auditorium: www.secc.co.uk (T) 0141 248 3000
Glasgow Botanic Gardens: www.glasgow.gov.uk (T) 0141 276 1614
University of Glasgow: www.gla.ac.uk (T) 0141 330 2000
Kelvingrove Art Gallery and Museum: www.glasgowlife.org.uk (T) 0141 276 9599
Glasgow Science Centre: www.gsc.org.uk (T) 0141 420 5000
Riverside Museum: www.glasgowlife.org.uk (T) 0141 287 2720
Titan Crane: www.titanclydebank.com (T) 0141 952 3771
Dumbarton Castle: www.historic-scotland.gov.uk (T) 01389 732167
Denny Tank, Dumbarton: www.scottishmaritimemuseum.org (T) 01389 763444